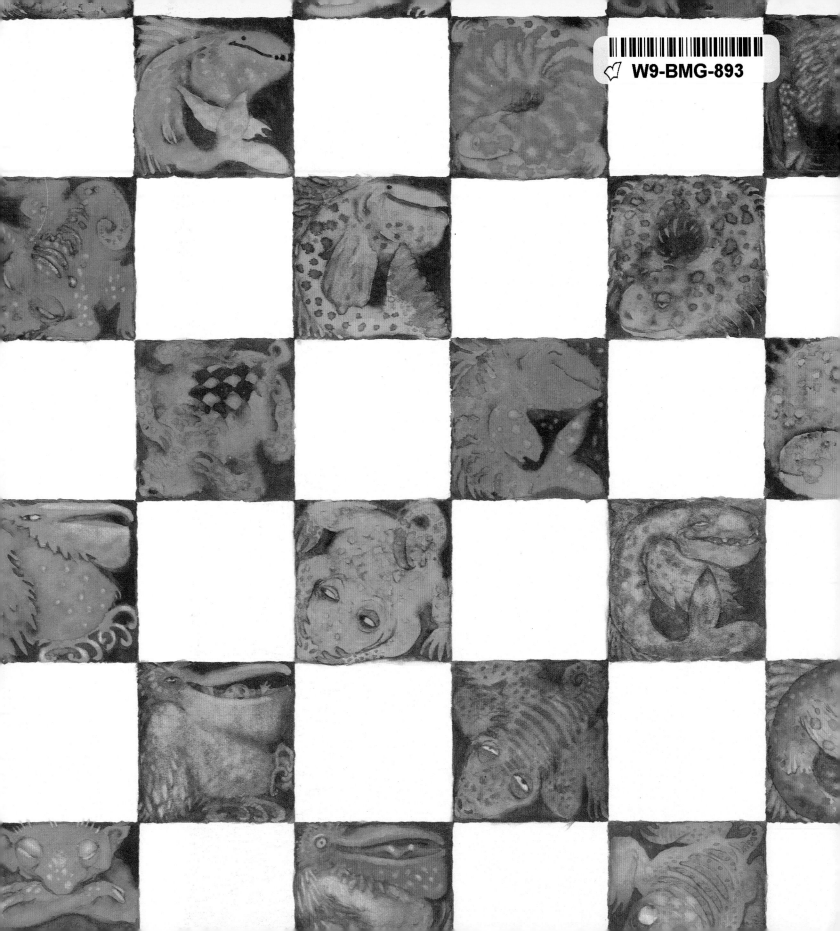

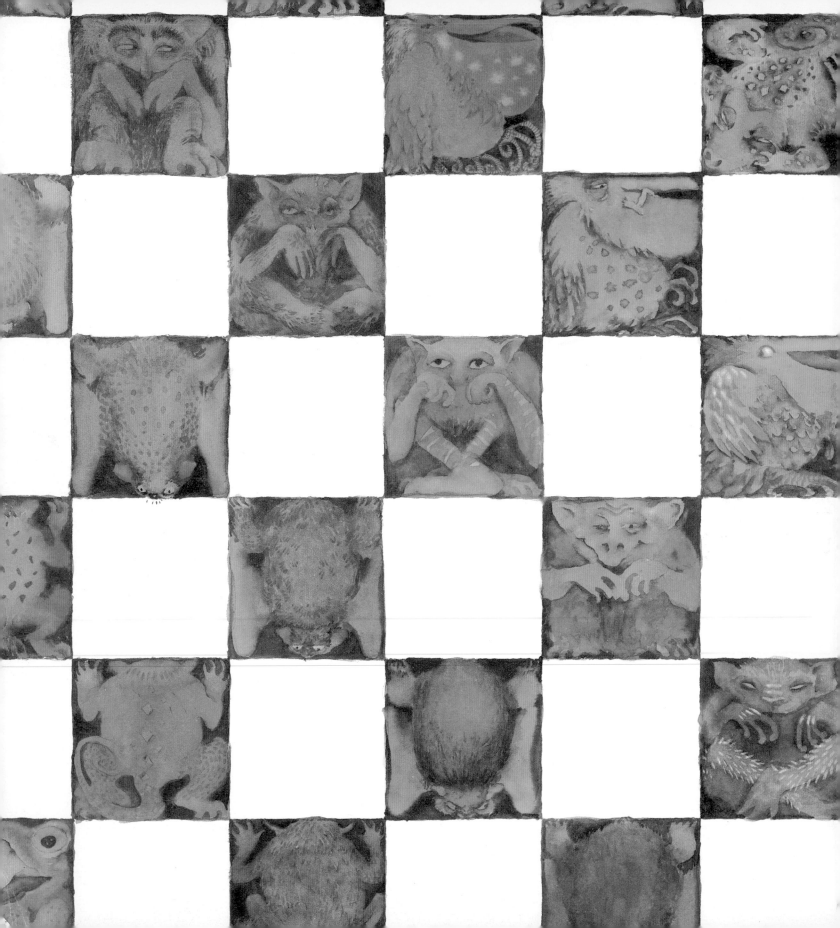

## A Note from the Compiler

Grateful acknowledgement to the copyright holders is hereby expressed for permission to reprint the following copyrighted material. Any errors or omissions are unintended and will be corrected in future printings.

"Hallowe'en" by Harry Behn. From *The Little Hill, Poems & Pictures* by Harry Behn. Copyright © 1949 by Harry Behn. Copyright © renewed 1977 by Alice L. Behn. Reprinted by permission of Marian Reiner.

"The Power Shovel" by Rowena Bennett. Copyright © 1948, © 1968 by Rowena Bennett. Reprinted by permission of Dr. Kenneth Bennett.

"What Night Would It Be?" by John Ciardi. From *You Read to Me, I'll Read To You* by John Ciardi. Copyright © 1962 by John Ciardi. Reprinted by permission of HarperCollins Children's Publishers.

"hist whist" by E.E. Cummings. Reprinted from *Hist Whist and other poems for children*, by E.E. Cummings, edited by George J. Firmage, by permission of Liveright Publishing Corporation. Copyright © 1923, 1944, 1949, 1950, 1951, 1953, 1958, 1961 by E.E. Cummings. Copyright © 1963 by Marion M. Cummings. Copyright © 1972, 1976, 1977, 1978, 1979, 1981, 1983 by the Trustees for the E.E. Cummings Trust. Reprinted in the United Kingdom by permission of the publishers, McGibbon & Kee, an imprint of HarperCollins Publishers Limited.

"I Like Fall," "Monsters," and "Scare Me Easy" by Beatrice Schenk de Regniers. From *A Bunch of Poems and Verses* by Beatrice Schenk de Regniers. Copyright © 1977 by Beatrice de Regniers. Reprinted by permission of Marian Reiner from the author.

"Thunder" by B.J. Lee. From *Poetry of Witches, Elves, and Goblins*. Selected by Leland B. Jacobs. Copyright © 1970, Garrard Publishing Company.

"Lullaby for Ugly Babies" and "Monster Soup" by Margo Lundell. Copyright © 1992 by Margo Lundell. Reprinted by permission of the author.

"Halloween Cats" by Jean Marzollo. Copyright © 1992 by Jean Marzollo. Reprinted by permission of the author.

"Bedtime Stories" by Lilian Moore. From *Spooky Rhymes and Riddles* by Lilian Moore. Copyright © 1972 by Lilian Moore. Reprinted by permission of Scholastic Inc.

"Ankylosaurus" by Jack Prelutsky. From *Tyrannosaurus Was a Beast* by Jack Prelutsky. Copyright © 1988 by Jack Prelutsky. Illustrations copyright © 1988 by Arnold Lobel. Published by Greenwillow Books and, in the United Kingdom, by Walker Books Limited. Reprinted by permission of Greenwillow Books, a division of William Morrow & Company, Inc., and Walker Books Limited.

"Giant" by Elizabeth Sawyer. Copyright © 1962 *The Instructor Magazine*. Reprinted by permission of Scholastic Inc.

"The Toaster" by William Jay Smith. From *Laughing Time* by William Jay Smith. Copyright © 1955, 1957, 1980, 1990 by William Jay Smith. Reprinted by permission of Farrar, Straus & Giroux

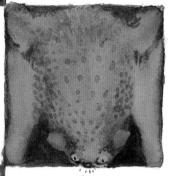

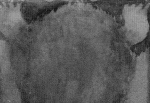

from **AN OLD CORNISH LITANY**
*Anonymous*

From Ghoulies and Ghosties
And long-leggity beasties
And all THINGS
That go BUMP in the night,
Good Lord, deliver us.

for she knows the devil          ooch
the devil          ouch
the devil
ach          the great

green
dancing
devil
devil

devil
devil

wheeEEE

## HIST WHIST

*e.e. cummings*

hist      whist
little ghostthings
tip-toe
twinkle-toe

little twitchy
witches and tingling
goblins
hob-a-nob     hob-a-nob

little hoppy happy
toad in tweeds
tweeds
little itchy mousies

with scuttling
eyes     rustle and run     and
hidehidehide
whisk

whisk     look out for the old woman
with the wart on her nose
what she'll do to yer
nobody knows

## LULLABY FOR UGLY BABIES
*Margo Lundell*

Lumpy babies
in a heap,
I beg you all
to go to sleep.

Rest my uglies,
rest in rows,
rest against
my tired toes.

Lean upon
my heart and chest.
Heaven knows,
I do my best.

## MONSTER SOUP
*Margo Lundell*

A beast as big
as half the sky
silently
began to cry:

"How dare these dragonettes
stay cool?
I'm nothing but
their swimming pool!

The pain in my poor jaw
is grim.
The sun beats down.
The dragons swim.

I need some shade.
I hope this group
soon finds the water
hot as soup.

Did I say soup?
My stomach's hollow.
Maybe I should simply…
swallow."

## HALLOWEEN CATS

*Jean Marzollo*

Cat monsters on the sidewalk,
Cat witches in the air,
Cat clowns on the doorstep,
Cat goblins in a chair.
Cat dancers in the doorway,
Cat knights at the door,
*Cat-o'-lanterns always watching,*
*Cat shadows on the floor.*

Cat monsters make a stir,
Cat witches take flight,
Cat clowns throw pies,
Cat goblins start a fight.
Cat dancers kick high,
Cat knights draw swords,
*Cat-o'-lanterns always watching,*
*Cat shadows on the floor.*

Cat monsters fall down,
Cat witches shrivel up,
Cat clowns fall asleep,
Cat goblins calm pup.
Cat dancers arabesque,
Cat knights take a bow,
*Cat-o'-lanterns always watching,*
*Cat shadows on the floor.*

BOO!

Tonight is the night
When leaves make a sound
Like a gnome in his home
Under the ground,
When spooks and trolls
Creep out of holes
Mossy and green.

Tonight is the night
When pumpkins stare
Through sheaves and leaves
Everywhere,
When ghoul and ghost
And goblin host
Dance round their queen.
It's Hallowe'en!

## HALLOWE'EN
*Harry Behn*

Tonight is the night
When dead leaves fly
Like witches on switches
Across the sky,
When elf and sprite
Flit through the night
On a moony sheen.

## I LIKE FALL

I like winter, spring, summer, and fall.
In the fall I like fall best of all.
    What I like most is
    A witch or a ghost is
Quite likely to pay me a call.

from **A BUNCH OF POEMS AND VERSES**
*Beatrice Schenk de Regniers*

## MONSTERS

Monsters do *not* scare me much,
Nor do goblins and ghosts and all such.
   But on Halloween night
    Please hold my hand tight—
I don't want to be out of touch.

## SCARE ME EASY

Scare me easy
Scare me slow
Scare me gentle
Don't let go
        my hand.

## WHAT NIGHT WOULD IT BE?
*John Ciardi*

If the moon shines
On the black pines
And an owl flies
And a ghost cries
And the hairs rise
On the back
  on the back
    on the back of your neck—

If you look quick
At the moon-slick
On the black air
And what goes there
Rides a broom-stick
And if things pick
At the back
  at the back
    at the back of your neck—

# ANKYLOSAURUS
*Jack Prelutsky*

Clankity Clankity Clankity Clank!
Ankylosaurus was built like a tank,
its hide was a fortress as sturdy as steel,
it tended to be an inedible meal.

It was armored in front, it was armored behind,
there wasn't a thing on its miniscule mind,
it waddled about on its four stubby legs,
nibbling on plants with a mouthful of pegs.

Ankylosaurus was best left alone,
its tail was a cudgel of gristle and bone,
Clankity Clankity Clankity Clank!
Ankylosaurus was built like a tank.

# THE POWER SHOVEL
*Rowena Bennett*

The power digger
Is much bigger
　　Than the biggest beast I know.
He snorts and roars
Like the dinosaurs
　　That lived long years ago.

He crouches low
　　On his tractor paws
And scoops the dirt up
　　With his jaws;
Then swings his long
　　Stiff neck around
And spits it out
　　Upon the ground.

Oh, the power digger
Is much bigger
　　Than the biggest beast I know.
He snorts and roars
Like the dinosaurs
　　That lived long years ago.

## THE TOASTER
*William Jay Smith*

A silver-scaled Dragon with jaws flaming red
Sits at my elbow and toasts my bread.
I hand him fat slices, and then, one by one,
He hands them back when he sees they are done.

## GIANT
*Elizabeth Sawyer*

One foot in the river,
  One foot in the lake—
What wonderful strides
  A giant can take!

The water goes "Squish"
  When he wiggles his toes.
Oh, giants have fun,
  As anyone knows.

His red rubber boots
  Reach up to his knee.
Why, puddles are nothing
  To giants like me!

## THUNDER
*B. J. Lee*

Do you know
What thunder is?
Beyond those clouds
So gray,
A giant's children
Slammed a door,
And skipped around
The sky to play
In quite a
Helter-skelter way.
So when you hear
The thunder, there
Are giant's children
In the air.

## BEDTIME STORIES
*Lilian Moore*

"Tell me a story,"
Says Witch's Child.

"About the Beast
So fierce and wild.

About a Ghost
That shrieks and groans.

A Skeleton
That rattles bones.

About a Monster
Crawly-creepy.

Something nice
To make me sleepy!"

# MONSTER SOUP
## AND OTHER SPOOKY POEMS

**Illustrated by Jacqueline Rogers**

**Compiled by Dilys Evans**

SCHOLASTIC INC.

New York   Toronto   London   Auckland   Sydney

Acknowledgements can be found on the last page.

ISBN 0-590-45209-6

Text compilation copyright © 1992 by Dilys Evans.
Illustrations copyright © 1992 by Jacqueline Rogers.
All rights reserved. Published by Scholastic Inc.

12 11 10 9 8 7 6 5 4 3 2 1                    2                    5 6 7 8 9/9 0/0

Printed in the U.S.A.                                                   08

# MONSTER SOUP
## AND OTHER SPOOKY POEMS

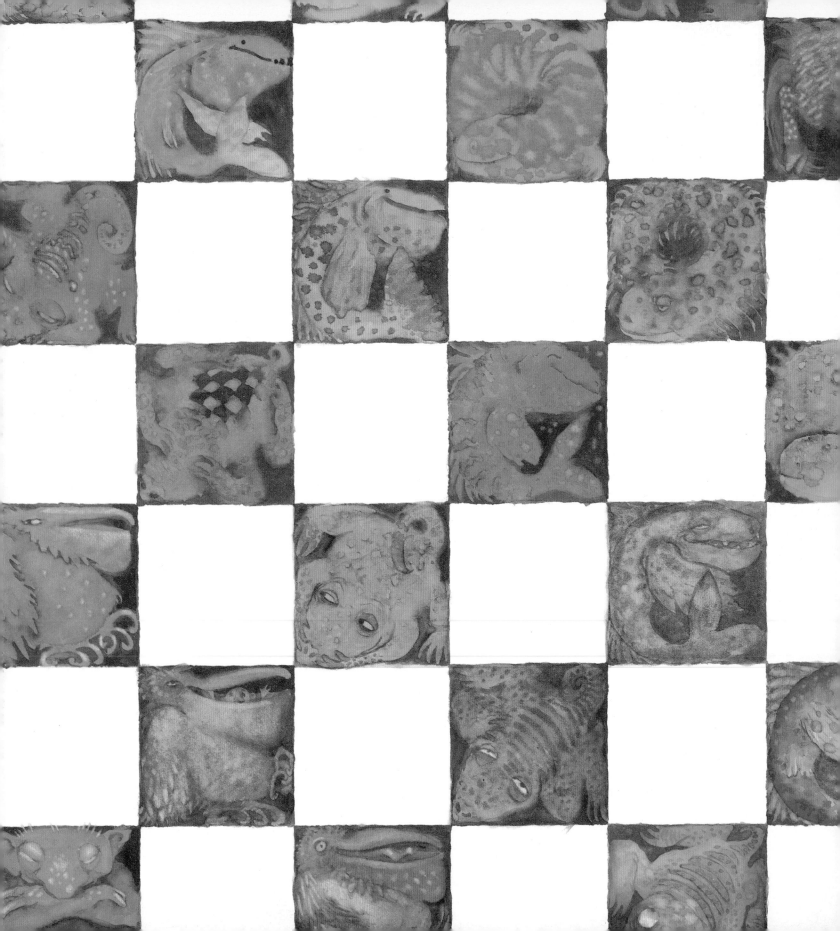